797,885 Books
are available to read at

Forgotten Books

www.ForgottenBooks.com

Forgotten Books' App
Available for mobile, tablet & eReader

ISBN 978-1-332-12531-9
PIBN 10288077

This book is a reproduction of an important historical work. Forgotten Books uses state-of-the-art technology to digitally reconstruct the work, preserving the original format whilst repairing imperfections present in the aged copy. In rare cases, an imperfection in the original, such as a blemish or missing page, may be replicated in our edition. We do, however, repair the vast majority of imperfections successfully; any imperfections that remain are intentionally left to preserve the state of such historical works.

Forgotten Books is a registered trademark of FB &c Ltd.
Copyright © 2015 FB &c Ltd.
FB &c Ltd, Dalton House, 60 Windsor Avenue, London, SW19 2RR.
Company number 08720141. Registered in England and Wales.

For support please visit www.forgottenbooks.com

1 MONTH OF FREE READING

at
www.ForgottenBooks.com

By purchasing this book you are eligible for one month membership to ForgottenBooks.com, giving you unlimited access to our entire collection of over 700,000 titles via our web site and mobile apps.

To claim your free month visit: www.forgottenbooks.com/free288077

* Offer is valid for 45 days from date of purchase. Terms and conditions apply.

Similar Books Are Available from
www.forgottenbooks.com

Marriage As It Is and As It Should Be
by John Bayley

Marriage and Family Life
A Jewish View, by Abraham B. Shoulson

When You Marry
by Evelyn Millis Duvall

African Systems of Kinship and Marriage
by A. R. Radcliffe-Brown

Marriage and Divorce
by John Haynes Holmes

The Physiology of Marriage
by Honore De Balzac

The Young Husband
Or Duties of Man in the Marriage Relation, by Wm. A. Alcott

The Emancipation of Women and Its Probable Consequences
by Adele Crepaz

An Enquiry Into the Duties of the Female Sex
by Thomas Gisborne

The Family Law of the Chinese
by Paul Georg Von Möllendorff

How to Pick a Mate
A Guidebook to Love, Sex and Marriage, by Dr. Clifford R. Adams

Is Marriage a Failure?
by Harry Quilter

Hints on Child-Training
by H. Clay Trumbull

The Control of Parenthood
by Arthur Thomson

Oriental Women
by Edward B. Pollard

Psychology and Parenthood
by H. Addington Bruce

What a Young Wife Ought to Know
Thousand Dollar Prize Book, by Mrs. Emma F. Angell Drake

Sex-Lore
A Primer on Courtship, Marriage, and Parenthood, by Mrs. S. Herbert

Life at Home
Or the Family and Its Members, by William Aikman

The Art of Taking a Wife
by Paolo Mantegazza

EUGENICS

By IRVING FISHER, Ph. D.

Professor of Political Economy, Yale University; Member Board of Scientific Directors, Eugenics Record Office

I HAVE SOMETIMES SAID THAT EUGENICS IS HYGIENE RAISED TO THE HIGHEST POWER. It is a comparatively new movement, but one which is sweeping over the world with wonderful rapidity, and taking hold of the emotions of mankind in a way that no other movement has ever done, or has deserved to do.

FIRST OF ALL, what is eugenics? Eugenics, as the Greek derivation of the word shows, means the science of right breeding. The word was invented by Sir Francis Galton, of England, to express his ideal founding a world movement to improve the human race. It was, of course, a colossal ambition, and, at first almost everybody scoffed. Even today there are comparatively few who realize how immediately practical is this dream of Sir Francis Galton's.

EUGENICS DOES NOT MEAN, as many people at first thought, anything like the old Spartan practice of infanticide. The Spartans tried to develop a strong, physical race according to their ideals, and they succeeded, but they did it in a cruel fashion by ruthlessly exposing children when born. Infanticide has been practiced in many of the barbarous countries of the world, and when eugenics was proposed, many people very naturally imagined this was what it meant. But it does not. Nor does eugenics propose to do violence in any other way to any humanitarian or Christian effort. Eugenics does not mean, as some have imagined, compulsory or government-made marriages. Some people have thought that eugenics was some half-baked scheme to breed the human race as we breed domestic animals, and to make a race of pug-noses or blond hair or blue eyes or any other fancy that some master of ceremonies should conceive. Nor does it mean a reduction in the proportion of love marriages. On the contrary, it means an increase of such marriages. Just as soon as men and women come to see and admire, as in ancient Greece, the ideal of physical perfection they will fall in love on that basis, as nature always intended that they should. There will be less interference with love marriages through ambition to acquire property or title.

Eugenics is simply an application of modern science to improve the human race. "But," says the skeptic, "that will take millions of years!" Nevertheless, I reassert that it is easily practical to alter and improve the human race and to do so in a very short time.

THIS IS THE NEW OPTIMISM OF EUGENICS and it is based on solid evidence. Until recently no one realized how fast the race *could* improve if it *would*. Even Galton himself, when he first proposed eugenics, was under the impression that we inherit from our ancestors in a way which would make possible improvement extremely slow. He put forward as a theory (what we now know to be incorrect) that each child gets half of its nature from its parents, one quarter from its grandparents, one-eighth from its great grandparents, one-sixteenth from its great great grandparents, and so on indefinitely back, the sum total of those fractions being, when added up to infinity, just unity or the whole inheritance. Instead of such a relation holding true, however, we know that a child inherits something from both parents in relation to every character of body or mind, and that the something which it inherits from its mother, as by its mother inherited from one (not both) of its mother's parents, and likewise the something which it inherited from the father, was inherited from one (not both) of the father's parents, and so on in two streams on either side, from each parent backward. Thus each individual today is in respect to any one characteristic (such, for example as eye-color) simply a combination of two beings in any previous generation. One generation back, it is the two parents from whom he gets his eye-color; two generations back it is two out of its four grandparents and not the other two at all; three generations back, it is two of its great grandparents and not the other six at all. Consequently, if you can carry back your inheritance to someone who came over in the Mayflower, the chances are a thousand to one, that you did not inherit any given character, such as eye-color, from that ancestor at all. In fact, you may have absolutely nothing in mind or body which came from him. The marvelous laws of inheritance are now being fairly well explained and understood. They were discovered first by a priest named Mendel, in the year 1869. But when he gave his discovery to the world, he found the world was blind and deaf, as it often is to new discoveries, and it waited until the beginning of the twentieth century, when DeVries and other scientists re-discovered the Mendelian principle, which today is the foundation stone of the science of heredity and eugenics.

WE CAN BEST UNDERSTAND MENDEL'S LAWS by taking a few concrete cases. The first case is that of an Andalusian fowl. We shall consider the two species, pure bred black and pure bred white and confine ourselves to observing the inheritance of the single characteristic, *color*. Of course, as long as the black mate only with the black their children will be black and as long as the white mate with white the children will be white. But if a white mates with a black, the children will not be either black or white, but blue. All will be blue. But the most interesting facts appear in the next generation when these hybrid blue fowls mate with black or the white or with each other. The original of the cross between the white and the black is an entirely new color, blue, which may be considered a sort amalgam of black and white. But a cross between the blue and the black will not be any new color, but will be either black or blue—and the chances are even. That is, in the long run about half of the children of blue and black parents will be blue and half will be black. None of the children will be white. So also crossing the blue with the white will result in half of the children being blue and half white. Still more curious is the result of mating blue with blue. One might imagine that in this case all the children would be blue, but only half will be blue, while a quarter will be black and a quarter white.

THESE LAWS SEEM STRANGE but at bottom they are simply the familar laws of chance, the laws which rule heads and tails in coin tossing. Two parents are like two baskets or bundles of traits from which the child takes its traits at random. In the wonderful play of Maeterlinck's, called the "Bluebird," we are taken to the "land before birth," where the children are waiting to be born, having selected their parents to be. Of course, this is only a pleasant fancy, like the advice of Oliver Wendell Holmes to children to choose good grand parents, but it is a useful fancy which will help us to understand the laws of heredity. The child of the Andalusian fowl takes its color from its two parents on the same principle as a lottery in which it would take two beans, white or black as the case might be, from each of two baskets. Every individual is a sort of basket containing two beans, as it were. It took one of these two beans from each parent and will give one to each child.

Eugenics

WITH THIS PICTURE OF A BEAN LOTTERY before us it is very easy to understood how the colors of Andalusian fowls are inherited. When two black fowls mate the offspring must be black, because in this case each parent basket contains a pair of black beans so to speak, so that the child taking one black bean from each basket will necessarily have a black pair. For the same reason the child of two white fowls must be white. But when a black and white fowl mate the child takes a white bean from one parent and a black from the other, its own color being a resultant or amalgam of the two, which in the case of the Andalusian fowl makes blue. Since every such hybrid child has this same combination of a white and a black bean all of these hybrids are alike. All are blue. It is important to remember that this hybrid blue is only a sort of mechanical mixture of black and white, and that the black and white are still separate beans, as it were.

BUT NOW SUPPOSE A HYBRID OR BLUE FOWL to mate with a white. This means that the child takes from the white parent or basket one of the two white beans and from the blue parent or basket one of the two beans of which one is white and the other black; the bean taken from the first or white basket must be white, but that taken from the second or blue or hybrid basket may be either white or black. It is a lottery with an even chance of drawing white or black. In the long run half of the children will draw white and half black. Those which draw the white will, since they also drew white from the other parent, be wholly white, but those which drew the black will be blue, since they will have one black and one white bean. We see too that the white child is just as truly white as though it had not had a hybrid parent, for of the two elements or beans which the hybrid carried, the black one was left behind untaken. We see that the blue child is a hybrid exactly like its hybrid parent, and not any new kind of cross between the blue and the white. In short, the children of a blue and white are either the one or the other, and not a mixture. In the same way if a blue mates with a black, half of the children will be black and half blue.

FINALLY WE COME TO THE MATING OF A BLUE WITH A BLUE. Here the lottery is to pick a bean from two baskets, each basket containing a white and a black bean. When at random one is taken from either of these two baskets there is an even chance that the bean from the father is white or black and an even chance that the bean from the mother is white or black.

NOW, what is the chance that the child draws a white bean from both baskets? Evidently it is one chance in four; for there are four ways equally probable in which you can take these beans, viz.: (1) black from the father basket and black from the mother, (2) white from the father and white from the mother, (3) white from the father and black from the mother, (4) black from the father and white from the mother. So the children could draw both white once in four times, both black once in four, and a white and a black in the other two cases. And that is why from two blue Andalusian fowls, on the average you will have one-quarter of the children black, one-quarter white, and the other two-quarters, blue. Again let us stop to emphasize the fact that the black children of these hybrids are just as pure blooded as their black grandparent, and will mate with other pure-blooded black in exactly the same way as though there had never been any white in their ancestry. The white strain has been left behind, or been "bred out."

WE HAVE SPOKEN OF ONE CHARACTER or characteristic— color. The same laws apply to other characters. Often different characters are inherited quite independently of one another. Each of us is a basket or bundle of very many qualities, each quality being a little compartment of the basket with two beans in it. There is, as it were, a pair of beans for every unit trait, whether that trait relates to color, to musical ability, or to any one of hundreds of other kinds.

To SUMMARIZE THE LAWS OF INHERITANCE of the unit character called color in Andalusian fowl, we have really six ways in which we can consider the mating of the three colored fowls (black, white, blue): (1) black may mate with black, in which case all the offspring will be black, (2) white may mate with white in which case all the offspring will be white, (3) a black may mate with a white, in which case the offspring will all be blue—a hybrid containing both black and blue elements, (4) blue may mate with a black, in which case half the offspring will be pure bred black, and half hybrid blue, (5) a blue may mate with a white, in which case half the offspring will be white and half blue, (6) blue may mate with blue in which case a quarter of the offspring will be white, a quarter black and a half blue.

These results are the fundamental laws of Mendel. But the results are not always as clear as in the case of the Andalusian fowl. In that case the hybrids were not like either parent, but were a new color, blue, so that they were labeled at once and recognizable as hybrids—but this is not generally the case. Take, for instance, guinea pigs. What will be the result of mating an "albino" white with a black guinea pig? Quite exactly the same principle applies as in the case of the Andalusian fowl, but the principle is not as clear to see. All the offspring are hybrid, but they will not be blue: they will be black. They will look like the black parent, but they are different. The black color predominates; i. e., black is "dominant" over white, while the white recedes out of sight, or is "recessive." This hybrid black guinea pig is like the hybrid blue Andalusian fowl. It is a hybrid, a combination of white and black, but in the guinea pig the black covers up the white so that *nothing* in the color reveals the fact that it is a hybrid. Now if the hybrid black offspring of these black and white guinea pigs mate with each other, the result will follow exactly the same Mendelian law as applied to the Andalusian fowl. But this will not be so clear, because now we have two kinds of black instead of a black and a blue. One child in four will be white like the grandparent. One child in four will be *pure bred* black like the grandparent, and two out of the four will be *hybrid* black. So to the eye we shall simply have, out of four children, one white and three black. But those three black are not all alike. One is a thoroughbred and two are half-breeds.

But how then are we to distinguish between the one pure bred black, the thoroughbred, and the two blacks that are hybrids so that we can be sure which is which? The only way they can be distinguished is to wait to see what their offspring will be in the next succeeding generations. The one that is a thoroughbred will behave like a thoroughbred. For instance, if mated with white they will have nothing but black children. But if one that is hybrid black mate with one that is white only half of the children will be white; these white children reveal the fact that their black parent was a half breed. Then we can put a tag on that black parent. If proper tags are put on the blacks so as to distinguish between the pure blooded and the half blooded—say a blue tag on the hybrids and a black on the thoroughbreds,—we shall get exactly the same results as described in the case of the Andalusian fowl, in the six cases mentioned. The same principles apply to qualities of guinea pigs other than color. Thus if a long-haired guinea pig mates with a short-haired guinea pig, all the offspring will be short-haired, because short hair is dominant over long hair. Again if a smooth coated guinea pig mates with a rough coated one the result will be rough coated, because a rough coat is dominant over a smooth coat.

By means of this Mendelian law it is thus possible to predict what will happen in various cases, not only for animals but for plants, and not only for the lower animals but for man himself. Mendel made his experiments mostly with plants. He took garden peas, twenty-two varieties. He crossed them and he found that when he crossed a wrinkled pea with a smooth pea all the children were smooth, but they were hybrids. They did not show any difference from one of the two parents. They showed a difference from the others, but they were hybrids nevertheless. They were not really thoroughbred smooth peas, but they were hybrid smooth peas. Then he mated these hybrid smooth peas with each other and the peas in the next generation were one-quarter wrinkled and three-quarters smooth, but he discovered that of those three-quarters only one-quarter was really smooth in the sense that it would breed true ever after. The others were hybrids and bred just like their parents. Again he took peas which were tall and mated them with peas that were dwarfed and he found that all the children were tall.

In other words, the character of being smooth was dominant and the character of being wrinkled was recessive, while likewise the character of being tall was dominant and the character of being dwarf was recessive.

Again he took peas according to the color of the flower—those that had purple flowers and those that had white flowers, and he found that purple was dominant over white. When the two were crossed the children would be all purple, but hybrid purple. If these hybrid purples were mated with each other, he found that one-quarter of the next generation would show white again according to the Mendelian law; one-quarter would be thoroughbred purple, and one-half would be hybrid purple. And so he worked with a number of other varieties of peas and other plants.

T̲HE VARIOUS CHARACTERS OF ROUGH OR SMOOTH, long haired or short haired, white or black, etc., are inherited independently of one another. That is to say, the child takes from the mystic baskets one pair of beans relative to color, another relative to hair length, another relative to coat, and so on, so that it may be, for instance, long haired and rough coated, long haired and smooth coated, short haired and rough coated, or short haired and smooth coated.

This independent inheritance does not always hold true. Sometimes two traits always go together or always avoid each other. Again, a particular trait may be dominant to another trait but recessive to a third, or dominant in the male and recessive in the female. Each case must be studied by itself, but when the rule is found it can be depended on and used to predict what will happen in other like cases.

T̲HESE LAWS ARE A CURIOUS MIXTURE of chance and certainty. In certain circumstances, as we have seen, we can predict with certainty that the offspring will be black, white, blue, or whatever the case may be. In other circumstances we can only state what the *chances* are. But these chances can be definitely stated as one in two, one in four or whatever it may be, and where there are large numbers of offspring this amounts to a practical certainty that definite proportions will have this or that color or other characteristics.

Evidently such definite knowledge can be made useful, and it has been made useful in England. Professor Biffen has created, to order as it were, in accordance with specifications drawn up officially, certain new and valuable species of wheat. This he did by crossing existing species so as to get "hybrids" without the undesirable qualities and with the desirable ones. One species of wheat is resistant to "rust," another has a stout stalk, another is beardless, another bears a large number of grains on a stalk, another a large yield per acre, but until Professor Biffen created it, no species possessed all these possibilities. By successive crossing of the existing species, however, he finally obtained species possessing all of these desirable qualities. Moreover, the desirable qualities were permanent because the other or undesirable qualities had been "bred out."

THE SAME MENDELIAN PRINCIPLES undoubtedly apply to the human race, although as yet only a few traits have been carefully studied. Eye color is one of these. Imagine a marriage of a thoroughbred, black-eyed Italian with a thoroughbred, blue-eyed Irish. What will be the result? All the children will be black-eyed, black being dominant over blue; but these black eyes are not the genuine article that the Italian parent possessed. They are a blend, and it is only because the black element dominates over or conceals the blue element that we cannot see on the surface that there is any blue there. But it may come out in the next generation; for, if these half-blooded individuals marry among themselves one-quarter of their children on the average will be blue-eyed. The other three-quarters will be black-eyed, but only one-quarter will be "really and truly" black-eyed, i. e., black-eyed like the Italian. The remaining half are hybrid black, like the parents. It is only a sort of imitation black, so to speak.

The appearance of blue eyes in the second generation is the long observed but formerly mysterious "atavism," or reversion to the grandparent.

NEXT, SUPPOSE THE CHILDREN OF AN ITALIAN AND AN IRISH PARENT intermarry with pure bred Italians. We immediately know what will be the result. All the children will be black-eyed, but among a large number only half will be thoroughbred black-eyed. The other half will be "imitation" black-eyed. The case is just like the mating of hybrid black guinea pigs with thoroughbred black guinea pigs, or of the blue fowl with the black. Similarly if the Irish-Italian hybrids marry with pure Irish, half the offspring will be blue-eyed and half will be hybrid black-eyed.

Black eyes are "dominant" over blue eyes because the black color is due to a pigment while the blue color is due to the absence of this pigment. In general a quality which is due to the presence of some positive element is dominant over a quality due to the absence of that element. A child inheriting from a blue-eyed person simply draws a blank from that side in the lottery.

THE CASE OF SKIN COLOR in human beings is more complicated. The skin color of an African is, according to the findings of Doctor Davenport, not a unit character but due to *four* factors. Without going into detailed explanations it follows, and the facts seem to substantiate the conclusion, that (1) the children (mulattos) of a white and a black parent have two color factors; and will all be of the same color midway between the colors of the parents; (2) the children of *two* mulattos will still be mulatto; (3) the offspring (quadroon) of a mulatto and a white will have *one* color factor and will all be alike midway between the parents, thus bringing us to a unit character. (4) The children of two quadroons will be quadroons; (5) the children (octoroons) of a quadroon and a white will be all quadroon color but getting this color from only one side and drawing a blank as it were from the other side, they will be quite different from the true quadroons so that (6) of the children of two octoroons, one-quarter will be white, one-quarter quadroons and a half octoroons, like the parents; (7) of the children of octoroons and white half will be octoroon and half will be white.

It is to be noted that when a white octoroon appears the black element has disappeared completely so that there is no danger of its reappearance in later generations from marriage with Caucasians. This does not mean, however, that all negro characteristics such as wooly hair, flat noses or thick lips, will disappear.

But, you say, what has all this to do with eugenics, and what difference does it make whether eye color or even skin color is one thing or another? It makes very little difference, indeed, but there are certain qualities that are exceedingly important. There are certain qualities which rank as defective. Feeble mindedness is a lack of a very important character. Suppose now that a normal or "strong minded" person, if we may use that term as distinct from feeble-minded, marries a feeble-minded person. Assuming that the "strong-minded" person is a "thoroughbred," all of the children will be apparently normal. None will be feeble-minded. "Strong-mindedness" is dominant over weak mindedness. Yet all these children that seem to be perfectly normal lack something in their bodies. This deficiency is simply covered up but can crop out in later generations. If two of these hybrids between the weak-minded and the strong-minded marry each other, one-quarter of the children will be feeble-minded, one-quarter thoroughbred strong-minded and the remaining half, though apparently strong-minded, will carry the taint in them just as their parents did. They are half-breeds. On the other hand, if two feeble-minded people marry, all of the children will be feeble-minded. Certainly we can and ought to forbid and prevent such marriages.

But feeble-mindedness is a recessive quality, so that if the feeble-minded marry only with normal individuals the feeble-mindedness does not blight the next generation, and if these apparently normal children of such marriages take pains to marry only really normal individuals, avoiding not only the feeble-minded but even those like themselves who have feeble-mindedness on one side of their family tree, there will be no feeble mindedness cropping out in future generations. The same observations apply to deaf mutism and some other defects.

BUT NOT ALL HUMAN ABNORMALTIES ARE RECESSIVE. Thus Huntington's chorea is dominant, so that every child of the unfortunate victim of this malady will contract it when it reaches the right age. Marriages of such people should, therefore, never be allowed, even with normal individuals.

But when we propose to restrict marriages or mating of those unfit to marry, people are apt to say, "That is a dream. It can't be done." But it can be done and it has been done. Every one has heard of the cretins in Switzerland. They are a kind of idiot who are short in stature and afflicted in all cases with goitre in the neck. Of course, many people have goitre who are not cretins, but there is no cretin who has not goitre. These cretins are peculiarly a feeble-minded people. They are common still in many towns of Switzerland; they are loathsome objects, helpless as children, with silly smiles, unable to take care of themselves in even the simplest toilet ways, and have to be looked after like domestic animals, or even more closely.

A GENTLEMAN VERY MUCH INTERESTED IN EUGENICS visited Aosta, in Italy, just outside of Switzerland once in 1900 and again in 1910. In 1900 he found many of these creatures among the beggars in the streets, in the asylum, in the home, in the orphan asylum—everywhere he ran across these awful apologies for human beings. But in 1910 he found only one! What had happened? Simply that a few resolute intelligent reformers had changed the entire situation. An isolation institution, or rather *two* institutions, one for the men and the other for the women, were established. In these the best care of the inmates was taken as long as they lived, and they do not live long. But pains were taken to see that by no possibility could marriage or mating of those people take place. They forfeited any such rights in return for the care that they received from the State.

Thus is it possible to apply the laws of heredity as laid down by Mendel in a thoroughly practical way and to get results *immediately* in one short generation. It seems, and it is, a colossal task to change average human nature one iota. Yet in the light of modern eugenics we could make a new human race in a hundred years if only people in positions of power and influence would wake up to the paramount importance of what eugenics means. And this could be done quietly and simply without violence to existing ideas of what is right and proper. It could be done by segregation of the sexes for defectives, feeble-minded, idiots, epileptics, insane, etc. By this kind of isolation, we can save the blood stream of our race from a tremendous amount of needless contamination.

And it is being done. The growing tendency to put defectives in institutions, though originally with no such object, will have the effect of reducing the transmission of defects, especially when it is recognized that the sexes must be separated and that the inmates should be kept at the institution through the reproductive period of life.

STERILIZATION IS ALSO A MEANS which may be advantageously applied in extreme cases. Sensible marriage laws if backed by an enlightened public opinion can add much. Every State should have a eugenics board authorized to pass on doubtful cases. But eugenic laws should be enacted only after approval by those who possess technical knowledge on this subject, such as Doctor Davenport. Otherwise we are in danger of foolish, needless and even harmful legislation.

FEW PEOPLE have any idea, unless they have looked into the pedigrees of some of these people, what awful contamination can be saved the race by a wise application of eugenics. There is a family called "the Jukes," all descended from a thriftless fisherman, born in 1720. About twelve hundred of these descendants have been traced in 75 years. Of these, 310 were professional paupers who spent an aggregate of 2,300 years in poorhouses, 50 were prostitutes, 7 murderers, 60 habitual thieves and 130 common criminals. Dugdale, who compiled these facts, estimated that the "Juke" family cost the Government over $1,000 for each member of the family. Similarly the "Tribe of Ishmael," numbering 1,692 individuals in six generations, has produced 121 known prostitutes and has bred hundreds of petty thieves, vagrants and murderers. Compare the descendants of that family with the descendants of Jonathan Edwards, who was born in the same period (1703) and who has had about the same number of descendants (1,394 traced up to 1900). Out of those descendants, something like half have been public men or men of great distinction and good influence in the world; 295 were college graduates, about 100 were clergymen or missionaries, over 100 were lawyers, 80 held public office, 75 were officers in the army or navy, 60 were eminent writers, 30 were judges, 13 were college presidents. A similar example is afforded in the Darwin family, of which, by the way, Galton was a member. There can be no doubt that human heredity plays a large rôle in human character.

A striking example of the contrast between good and bad heredity is afforded by two sets of descendants from the same man. An English soldier, a well endowed man, married twice. His first wife was feeble-minded, his second, a normal woman. Records of the descendants show a taint of feeble-mindedness running through the children of the first marriage and none whatever among the children of the second.

THE SUBJECT OF EUGENICS IS INTIMATELY RELATED TO HYGIENE. Some people have thought that hygiene is opposed to eugenics, and in truth this may in many cases be true. Misapplied hygiene is likely to be injurious to the race. I was astonished at the ignorance of a university president with whom I conversed some years ago. He was very enthusiastic over hygiene and what it can do. He said, "I know of a girl who had many ailments and disabilities. She had a surgical operation to remedy one difficulty and special treatment to remedy others, so that finally she was so repaired and improved as to be made over into quite a respectable human being, *and now she is married*. Just think what a wonderful thing that is." Well the truth was such a result is greatly to be deplored. The hygiene was misapplied. This girl was really defective, and the pity of it is that her children and grandchildren and great grandchildren are likely to have a certain percentage of defects. The lives of the insane of this country have been prolonged about eight years by hygiene. To a certain extent this prolongation has done harm because the insane have been allowed to breed. In Connecticut there was a half-witted woman in an asylum, and a farmer near by, who was also half-witted but was not in the asylum, asked to marry her. The keeper of the institution actually did not know any better than to say, "Why, of course, I will be glad to get rid of her support." And so they married, and in the course of another generation, both of them came back to the institution with seven idiotic children! When the superintendent got rid of the woman's support it was a "penny wise and pound foolish" economy.

But hygiene need not interfere with and may supplement eugenics. Eugenics is simply the hygiene of future generations.

There are two special points of contact between hygiene and eugenics which ought to be mentioned. One is in relation to alcohol. Experiments with hens and with guinea pigs have shown that merely inhaling fumes of alcohol spoils the germ plasm and a large percentage of the children of the animals that have been affected by alcohol have been deformed. The chickens and the guinea pigs that come from alcoholic ancestry will be, according to the Mendelian laws, deformed. Now we cannot experiment with human beings, but we can observe (and Forel, in Switzerland, and others have made observations which, if they do not prove, certainly make it reasonably certain to any fair minded man or woman) that the alcoholic taint can and does affect the germ plasm of which future generations are made. It is unreasonable to infer that any unhygienic habits, even bad diet, may to some extent disturb the germ plasm.

THE OTHER POINT OF CONTACT betewen hygiene and eugenics is called "social hygiene." One of the two great diseases associated with immorality is inherited and the other may also blight the child's health, especially as to eye sight. It is an awful thing to think that any human being can take the responsibility or run the risk of cursing future generations. Half of the infantile congenital blindness of the world today comes about in this way. I knew of a young man who married and had one normal child. But the second child was born blind. His doctor explained it to him, that not all who thought themselves cured of this disease which he had contracted as a young man are really cured. As to that disease one can never be sure whether he is cured or not. In talking to young men on this subject, I find that the best appeal to them is the eugenic appeal. It does not always work to tell a young man to refrain from immorality because of the danger to himself. He may take that as a "dare." Besides it does not put the subject on a sufficiently high plane. It must be explained to him that it is wrong and it must be explained to him why it is wrong. Now it is fundamentally wrong because he carries within his body the germ plasm of which he is the custodian for future generations. It does not belong to him. It is not for him to risk or to injure. It is something that he carries in trust; it is something he must guard as the most precious possession possible. He must be on the side of morality because that is being on the side of the human race. It is easy to get a young man interested in the white slave traffic and to get him interested to fight the white slave traffic. As soon as he is interested enough he begins to see that he cannot be on both sides at once. If he wants to fight the under world he must not become a traitor to the side for which he is fighting, and patronizing the underworld is disloyalty of the rankest kind,—the disloyalty to his own family, his own home, as well as to the institution of the family and the home. I say to young men, "When you are married men you expect to be faithful and true. You would not respect your father if he were not faithful to your mother. Carry this a step farther: when you are engaged, and even before you are engaged, you should hold it as a matter of honor and of true fidelity to be just as faithful as after you are married. Another step: before you are engaged, you owe it to the girl you are going to get engaged to, to do for her what you would expect her to do for you, namely, to bring to her a pure body. You may not know who she is, but she is now living somewhere and reserving herself for you." It is easy to get young men to see that the double standard is false and that only the true and old-fashioned ten commandment morality is right.

THIS LEADS ME TO SAY THAT EUGENICS IS A WONDERFUL TOUCHSTONE. I believe eugenics will be in the future the essential foundation of ethics. Today, ethics is purely empirical. We teach at the mother's knee certain things to be right and certain things to be wrong, and they generally are right and wrong respectively. And yet we cannot explain *why* they are right and wrong. When the children ask us "Why?" we usually put them off by saying "Because it is right," or we put young men off by metaphysics and say, "Because of the catagorical imperative," as Kant expressed it. But this does not satisfy, and the failure to satisfy is one reason for immorality in the world. There is not yet an accepted scientific foundation for right and wrong. I verily believe that eugenics is going to supply such a foundation. Some people say they don't think eugenics is right; they don't think it is right to talk about these things; they don't think that it is right to try to interfere with marriage. There are many things these people don't think is right because they have a false and conventional standard. But the time will come when, instead of asking whether eugenics is right or wrong according to some false conventional standard, we shall ask ourselves whether these conventional standards are right or wrong according to the standard of eugenics, the highest standard there is.

AND SO IT WILL SOME DAY COME ABOUT that we shall realize the dream of the founder of this science, Sir Francis Galton, and will link up eugenics with religion. A generation ago much was said of the conflict between science and religion; and it is a curious fact that at first religion frowned on new scientific discoveries. It frowned on the discovery of the rotundity of the earth, of the motion of the earth, of the geological periods of evolution according to Darwin, and of a great many other things. Some of the greatest saints in science, like Galileo and Bruno, were imprisoned and tortured because they would not prostitute their love of truth for the conventional religion of the day. Now I was fearful at first that we should have another unpleasant spectacle of a conflict between conventional religion and this new science of eugenics, and if you will watch the newspapers as I have been watching them during the last year, you will see occasional evidences of that today. One of the evidences of it came to me some years ago when David Starr Jordan, President of Leland Stanford University, and I both spoke before the New York Peace Society. We talked about the relation of eugenics to war. President Jordan showed that war was non-eugenic and therefore wrong. War is wrong today because it takes the very best young men who ought to be the fathers of the next generation and makes them targets for the bullets of our neighbors. War is thus a cause of degeneration. The Napoleonic Wars were largely responsible, President Jordan thought, for the reduction in stature of the French. The tall men were sent to war.

AFTER WE HAD FINISHED our presentation of the subject a clergyman got up and said, "I disagree with the gentlemen who have spoken; men and women are not bred like sheep." This clergyman condemned at once the ideas we stood for because he had a narrow theological dogma that was impeding in his brain the reception of a new idea. But I am glad to note that such men are exceptional today. There is no conflict in evidence, except in very rare cases, between science and eugenics. On the contrary, for once in the history of the world, religion is accepting with open arms this eugenics as a new ally for morality. Dean Sumner was one of the first to link up religion with eugenics when he proclaimed in Chicago that in his church there would thereafter be no marriages solemnized unless the contracting parties should come prepared with statements from physicians showing that they were fit to be parents of the human race. Since he did that, hundreds of clergymen and scores of clerical bodies and scientific bodies have passed resolutions favoring such a measure.

SOME PEOPLE ALTOGETHER MISS THE POINT OF THIS RELIGIOUS SANCTION of eugenic marriages. It is not that it will prevent any persons from getting married who wish to outrage eugenic laws. They can easily find plenty of places where they can get married without medical certificates. But the fact that religion approves of eugenic marriages and disapproves of non-eugenic marriages will *reform public opinion* and ultimately make unsuitable marriages as incident as incest is today. This public opinion when it is full grown will not be simply a dull and lazy approval of eugenics, but a religious fervor. We shall make of eugenics the biggest pillar of the church, and eugenics will become embedded in the religion of the future. It shall happen hereafter that instead of conflicts between science and religion, these two great human interests will be marching together, hand in hand.

PROCEEDINGS
The National Conference on Race Betterment

THE National Conference on Race Betterment which convened at Battle Creek January 8th to 12th, marked a new era in human welfare work. At this meeting there came together leaders in the various movements represented by sociology, eugenics, biology, physiology, psychology, education, etc. Among those present were Dr. C. B. Davenport, Director of the Carnegie Station of Experimental Evolution; Rev. Newell Dwight Hillis; Hon. Jacob Riis, head of the Jacob Riis Neighborhood Settlement, New York; Judge Ben Lindsey of the Denver Juvenile Court; Prof. Graham Taylor, President of the Chicago School of Civics and Philanthropy; Dr. Winfield Scott Hall, Professor of Physiology in the Northwestern University; Mr. Frederick L. Hoffman, Statistician of the Prudential Life Insurance Company; Mr. E. E. Rittenhouse, Conservation Commissioner of the Equitable Life Insurance Company; Dr. J. N. Hurty, Secretary of the Indiana State Board of Health; Dr. D. A. Sargent, Harvard University; Mr. Arthur Hunter, Actuary of the New York Life Insurance Company.

The program covered every field of welfare endeavor and brought out information that will make possible a basis for a broader, more intelligent, more efficient social program for the future.

Proceedings of the Conference have been published in full. The volume comprises a mine of practical information that should be available not only to every social worker, but to every person interested not only in his own welfare, but in that of his neighborhood. Price one dollar.

Address,
GOOD HEALTH PUBLISHING CO.,
Battle Creek, Mich.

RETURN TO the circulation desk of any
University of California Library

or to the

NORTHERN REGIONAL LIBRARY FACILITY
Bldg. 400, Richmond Field Station
University of California
Richmond, CA 94804-4698

ALL BOOKS MAY BE RECALLED AFTER 7 DAYS

- 2-month loans may be renewed by calling (510) 642-6753
- 1-year loans may be recharged by bringing books to NRLF
- Renewals and recharges may be made 4 days prior to due date

CPSIA information can be obtained at www.ICGtesting.com
Printed in the USA
LVOW10s1436200416

484518LV00041B/883/P